UN Peace Operations

Part III

Effectiveness of UN Peace Operations: Dynamics of Composition of Troops and Diversity on UN Peace Operations

UN Peace Operations

Part III

Effectiveness of UN Peace Operations: Dynamics of Composition of Troops and Diversity on UN Peace Operations

Edited by

A K Bardalai and Pradeep Goswami

(Established 1870)

A Joint USI - ICWA Publication

Vij Books India Pvt Ltd
New Delhi (India)

Published by

Vij Books India Pvt Ltd
(Publishers, Distributors & Importers)
2/19, Ansari Road
Delhi – 110 002
Phones: 91-11-43596460, 91-11-47340674
Mob: 98110 94883
e-mail: contact@vijpublishing.com
web : www.vijbooks.in

First Published in India in 2021

ISBN: 978-93-90917-68-6

Contents

Preface

India's deepening engagement with the United Nations (UN) is based on its steadfast commitment to multilateralism and dialogue as the key for achieving shared goals and addressing common challenges faced by the global community. These include those related to peacebuilding and peacekeeping, sustainable development, poverty eradication, environment, climate change, terrorism, disarmament, human rights, health and pandemics, migration, cyber security, space and frontier technologies like Artificial Intelligence, comprehensive reform of the UN including the reform of the Security Council, among others.

India was among the select members of the UN that signed the Declaration by UN at Washington on 01 January 1942. India also participated in the historic UN Conference of International Organisation at San Francisco from 25 April to 26 June 1945. India strongly supports the purposes and principles of the UN. It has made significant contributions to implementing the goals of the Charter and the evolution of the UN's specialised programmes and agencies. India believes that the UN and the norms of international relations that it has fostered remain the most efficacious means for tackling today's global challenges. India is steadfast in its efforts to work with the comity of nations, in the spirit of multilateralism, to achieve comprehensive and equitable solutions to all problems facing us, including development and poverty eradication, climate change etc.

India has a long and distinguished history of service in UN peacekeeping, having contributed more personnel than any other country. To date, more than 253,000 Indians have served in 49 of the 71 UN peacekeeping missions established around the world since 1948. Currently, around 5,500 troops and police personnel from India are deployed in eight of 12 UN peacekeeping missions, the fifth-highest amongst troop-contributing countries.

Commencing with its participation in the UN operation in Korea in the 1950s, India's mediatory role in resolving the stalemate over prisoners of war in Korea led to the signing of the armistice ending the Korean War. India chaired the five-member Neutral Nations Repatriation Commission while the Indian Custodian Force supervised the process of interviews and repatriation that followed. The UN entrusted Indian Armed Forces with subsequent peace missions in the Middle East, Cyprus, and the Congo (since 1971, Zaire). India also served as chair of the three international commissions for supervision and control for Vietnam, Cambodia, and Laos established by the 1954 Geneva Accords on Indochina.

India has a long tradition of sending women on UN peacekeeping missions. In 2007, India became the first country to deploy an all-women contingent to a UN peacekeeping mission. Medical care, veterinary support to the domestic animals of the local population, and constructional activities are among the many services Indian peacekeepers provide to the communities in which they serve on behalf of the organisation.

India has provided a number of senior level mission leaders, including Head of the Mission, Force Commanders, Deputy Head of the Mission, Deputy Force Commanders and senior staff officers to various missions. Besides the

Force Commanders, India also had the honour of providing two Military Advisors, one woman Police Adviser and one Deputy Military Advisor to the Secretary-General of the UN. The first Indian all-women contingent in peacekeeping mission, a Formed Police Unit, was deployed in 2007 to the UN Mission in Liberia (UNMIL). India was the first country to contribute to the Trust Fund on Sexual Exploitation and Abuse, which was set up in 2016. India's longstanding service has not come without cost, hundreds of Indian peacekeepers have paid the ultimate price while serving with the UN. India has lost more peacekeepers than any other member state.

In the more than seven decades of UN peacekeeping operations, interventions in different kinds of conflict, peacekeepers always faced multiple challenges when it came to implementing the mandate. With the passage of time, these challenges have become more complex, undermining the ability of the peace operations to deliver in the conflict zone. This is also what the Department of UN Peace Operation's survey of August 2019 indicates. Besides the inherent lag between the intent and the outcome in all spheres of the activities, there could be several other strategic and operational reasons for slow progress of reforms in the field. This is not to conclude that so far no reform has taken place. India has been one of the oldest contributors in peacekeeping operations and, hence, is a vast repository of the best practices.

The United Service Institution (USI) of India in the past has taken the lead in providing the platform for organising discourse and research in the field of UN peace operations to put across an Indian perspective on few of the most crucial attributes of the current challenges that face reforms of the UN peace operations. At this juncture, USI of India (https://usiofindia.org), the oldest think tank in India, in collaboration with Indian Council of World Affairs (ICWA) (https://www.icwa.in), the premium think tank of India's Ministry of External Affairs, Government of India, planned to conduct a series of webinars on UN peace operations in 2021 on the following themes:

> Theme 1 - India and UN Peace Operations: Principles of UN Peacekeeping and Mandate.

> Theme 2 - UN Peace Operations: Hostage-taking of Peacekeepers.

> Theme 3 - Effectiveness of UN Peace Operations: Dynamics of Composition of Troops and Diversity on UN Peace Operations

> Theme 4 - UN Peace Operations: Protection of civilians.

> Theme 5 - Women, Peace and Security.

> Theme 6 - Interoperability Challenges in multidimensional Peace Operations: Role of Senior Mission Leaders (Head of the Mission and Force Commanders).

Inaugural UN webinar was conducted on 27 Feb 2021 on 'India and UN Peace Operations: Principles of UN Peacekeeping and Mandate'. A good comprehension of the meaning of the principles of peacekeeping is important because the way these are interpreted will continue to impact the performance of peace operations. Therefore, this should be the topic of discussion and debate as part of the pre-deployment training in the troop-contributing countries and post-deployment training in the mission area. This would help to reduce the scope of misinterpretation of the nuances of principles of peacekeeping and its impact on the effectiveness of the mission. Accordingly, the first webinar was held on the following sub-themes:

> Principles of UN Peacekeeping, its continued relevance and mandate implementation.

> Relevance of the principle of 'Use of Force' in United Nations Stabilisation Mission in Congo (MONUSCO) and United Nations Mission in South Sudan (UNMISS).

> Contribution of traditional peace operations [United Nations Interim Force in Lebanon (UNIFIL) and United Nations Disengagement Force (UNDOF)] for sustainable peace.

The second UN webinar was conducted on 29 Jun 2021 on 'UN Peace Operations: Hostage-taking of Peacekeepers'. Hostage-taking is not a new phenomenon. Even the ancient Romans took hostages of princes as a guarantee to the obligations made for their conquered regions. In medieval times, knights used to be taken hostage for ransom. Some would, however, like to use the word kidnap in place of a hostage. Whether hostage-taking or kidnapping, these are all part of extortionist terrorist acts and there is always a motive. This practice has flourished in contemporary times with the criminal gangs either for ransom or for forcing the hands of the authority to allow them to escape unharmed. Peacekeepers are supposed to be the enablers and get deployed in the conflict zone to help bring peace and save human lives. But when the peacekeepers themselves become the victims, would impact the effectiveness of the mission. Following a hard-line invariably invite retaliation. Response to a hostage crisis will depend on several variables which will have to be considered in the hostage rescue strategy. This webinar discussed two different situations necessitating two different approaches with the following sub-themes:

- ➤ Overview of the hostage crisis, its implications and tenets of rescue strategy.

- ➤ Emerging trends in hostage-taking of peacekeepers.

- ➤ Strategy & challenges of hostage rescue when peacekeepers from larger TCCs are taken hostage United Nations Mission in Sierra Leone (UNAMASIL).

- ➤ Strategy & challenges when peacekeepers from smaller TCCs are taken hostage (UNDOF).

The Third UN webinar was conducted on 25 Aug 2021 on "Effectiveness of UN Peace Operations: Dynamics of Composition of Troops and Diversity on UN Peace Operations". With the increasing number of intra-state conflicts and growing intensity of violence in the UN mission areas, effectiveness of UN peace operations have come under scrutiny. Despite the robustness of the mandate, the situations on the ground have not improved. Since the early 2010s, the underperformance of the UN peacekeeping operations has been the central focus of the UN Headquarters. The UN Secretariat initiated an attempt to develop the Comprehensive Performance Assessment System (CPAS) supported by the UN Security Council. The Secretary General's Action for Peacekeeping (A4P) initiative of 2018 also focuses only on the accountability of the UN military, police, and the force commander. Many of the countries in the Global South, specifically the TCCs, are of the view that the performance and accountability mechanism would be successful only when it covers all stakeholders and all phases of peacekeeping operations. They are also of the view that the responsibility of the Great Powers in the UN Security Council does not end with the generation of mandates. For instance, a representative stated that the "UN Security Council members should be held accountable if unachievable mandates are generated for political expediency or if adequate resources are not made available".

Diversity matters and affects peacekeeping effectiveness. Mission diversity and effectiveness are falsely assumed to be dichotomous. On the contrary, we can actually enhance effectiveness by increasing diversity. When Blue Helmets deploy in peacekeeping missions, they carry with them their operational ethos, the way they are trained and, cultures and traditions that are unique to different Troop Contributing Countries (TCCs). These characteristics shape the peacekeepers' approach to peacekeeping. Ultimately, assessment of peace operation must account for a range of factors, some of which are given in mandate and some of which are not. This reality presents peace operations with a significant challenge to mandate implementation. In this webinar, the discussion focused on the following sub-themes:

> Effect of composition of troops and diversity - Views of an academician.

> Effect of composition of troops and diversity - Perspective of a practitioner.

> Effects of cultural, social and military ethos - Perspective of an Indian contingent commander.

This monograph is a compilation of talks by eminent speakers during the third webinar on 'Effectiveness of UN Peace Operations: Dynamics of Composition of Troops and Diversity on UN Peace Operations'.

About the Participants

Major General BK Sharma, AVSM, SM (Retd)** is the Director of the USI of India, India's oldest think tank established by the British in 1870. He has tenanted prestigious assignments in India, including command of a mountain division on the China border and Senior Faculty Member at the National Defence College, New Delhi. He has represented his country at the UN as Military Observer in Central America and has been India's Defence Attaché in Central Asia. He specialises in Strategic Net Assessment methodology, Scenario Building and Strategic Gaming.

Ambassador Vijay Thakur Singh is the Director General (DG), ICWA, a premium think tank of the Ministry of External Affairs. She is a carrier diplomat and had multilateral experience, during her service with the Ministry of External Affairs, GOI. She was High Commissioner of India to Singapore and Ireland and prior to that, Joint Secretary to the President of India and Joint Secretary at the National Security Council Secretariat (NSCS). She also handled Afghanistan and Pakistan desk in the Ministry of External Affairs and was Counsellor in the Embassy of India in Kabul. She was also a Counsellor in the Permanent Mission of India to the United Nations in New York. She retired in September 2020 as Secretary (East), Ministry of External Affairs.

Ms Pernilla Rydén is the Director, Challenges Forum International Secretariat. She is a well-known UN professional, with more than 20 years of experience in different international settings to include several UN peace operations in Africa and Middle East (Yemen, Congo, Iraq, Kosovo, Sudan, Liberia), the EU civilian crisis management (CPCC) and the Organisation for Security Cooperation in Europe (OSCE) in Croatia. She has a number of publications and reports to her credit.

Major General PK Goswami, VSM (Retd) is the Deputy Director at the USI of India and Head of USI UN Cell. He is also the chief coordinator for series of USI – ICWA webinars on UN Peace Operations. He was Military Observer with United Nations Verification Mission at Angola (UNAVEM) in 1991-92 and Senior Faculty at National Defence College, New Delhi. He represented National Defence College, India, at the 16th ASEAN Regional Forum for Heads of Defence Universities, Colleges and Institutions in Beijing, China in November 2012.

Major General (Dr) AK Bardalai (Retd) is a Distinguished Fellow at the USI and an Indian Army veteran. He has held various command and staff assignments at different levels, including the command of an infantry division. He was also the Commandant of the Indian Military Training Team in Bhutan 2011 - 2014. He was a Military Observer in the United Nations Verification Mission in Angola (UNAVEM) in 1991- 92 and Deputy Head of the Mission and Deputy Force Commander of United Nations Interim Forces in Lebanon (UNIFIL) 2008 - 2010. He is the recipient of PhD for his research on UN Peace Operations from Tilburg University (the Netherlands). He has authored and co-authored books on UN Peace Operations and regularly contributes articles/papers on the issues.

Dr Chiara Ruffa is an associate professor at the Swedish Defence University and academy fellow at Uppsala University. Her research is about civil-military relations, peacekeeping operations, state militaries, norms and military cultures.

Her work has been published in the European Journal of International Relations, European Journal of International Security, Security Studies and Acta Sociologica among others. She is the author of "Military Cultures in Peace and Stability Operations" (University of Pennsylvania Press, 2018) and of "Composing Peace: Mission Composition in UN Peacekeeping" (with Vincenzo Bove and Andrea Ruggeri, Oxford University Press, 2020).

Colonel (Dr) KK Sharma (Retd) is a Visiting Fellow at the USI and an Indian Army veteran. He was a military observer in UNTAC, Cambodia in 1992 - 1993. He was an active member in planning and writing of UN Capstone Doctrine on peacekeeping and manuals for trainers in the Office of High Commissioner of Human Rights, Geneva. He has been associated with the planning cell of peacekeeping operations in Army HQ and was a founding member of starting Centre for UN Peacekeeping under the USI of India. He is PhD in Management from Zurich, Switzerland and presently a Professor and Dean, Global Education Programs in Chitkara University, responsible to mentor and administer UG courses in academic collaboration with the University of Windsor and Trent University, Canada.

Colonel Kaustubh Kekre is a serving Indian Army officer, presently heading Indian Centre for UN Peacekeeping at New Delhi, India. The officer had two stints on deputation with the United Nations. He was the Chief Logistics Staff Officer of a Sector in MONUSCO and then was a Contingent Commander of an Infantry Battalion Group in the same mission. The officer has attended the prestigious Defence Services Staff College Course at Wellington, Tamil Nadu and the Higher Command Course at Army War College, Mhow.

Concept Note

Effectiveness of UN Peace Operations

In its 76 years of history, the efficacy of UN peace operations remain mixed. The failures of Rwanda, Somalia or former Yugoslavia have always been cited to criticise the conduct of UN peacekeeping. Authors and critics conveniently ignore many laudable successes and its unique contribution to the conflict management in many such complex operations. To enhance the effectiveness of the UN peace operations, the UN, however, has tried to introduce several reforms over the last 30 years. In evaluating the UN peacekeeping, the analysts tend to confuse Effectiveness and Success in the context of a peacekeeping operation, success can be defined as achieving the mission mandate, which can be measured. On the other hand, effectiveness is the capability of producing a desired result or output. According to some behavioural scientists, trying to make the distinction seems like 'splitting hairs' as both words can be used interchangeably. To enhance the effectiveness, it is also important to have a better understanding of why a particular UN peace operation succeeds or fails. Several strategic and organisational specific variables can impact the performance of an UN peace operation, which are not homogeneous. Intangibles also include peacekeepers drawn from many TCCs with different military doctrines, cultural and societal backgrounds, operational ethos and proclivity towards mandate implementation. One of the most important factor that impacts the performance at operational level is the composition of the mission in terms of peacekeeping contingents, including police personnel.

There is a need to analyse characteristics of contingents and their operational behavioural patterns. This can lead one to assess as to how does the composition of peacekeeping contingents from Western and non-Western nations in a traditional mission like UNIFIL, or in a complex mission with mixed contingents (Asians and Africans) in Congo (MONUSCO), or the African contingents in The United Nations Multidimensional Integrated Stabilization Mission in Mali (MINUSMA) influence the performance in these operations? An assessment of the said aspect can help optimum utilisation of the varying capabilities of different peacekeeping contingents and bring in new perspectives to the pre-induction training to fulfil the mandate.

In this webinar on the 'Effectiveness of UN peace operations: Dynamics of Composition of Troops and Diversity on UN Peace Operations' was discussed as under:

(a) Effect of Composition of Troops and Diversity - Views of an Academician.

(b) Effect of Composition of Troops and Diversity - Perspective of a Practitioner.

(c) Effects of Cultural, Social and Military Ethos - Perspective of an Indian Contingent Commander.

Introductory Remarks

Major General PK Goswami, VSM (Retd)

At the outset, on behalf of Maj Gen BK Sharma, Director, USI and Amb Vijay Thakur Singh, Director General, ICWA, I welcome all participants to today's webinar.

I am glad to inform you that this year the USI, in collaboration with ICWA, is conducting a series of webinars on UN related issues. Inaugural webinar, conducted on 27 Feb 2021 on **'Principles of UN Peace Keeping and Mandate'**, was followed by **'The Impact of Climate Change on UN Peacekeeping Operations'** on 20 Apr 2021 in collaboration with NUPI & SIPRI and **'UN Peace Operations: Hostage taking of UN Peacekeepers'** on 29 June 21. Today we will deliberate on **'Effectiveness of UN Peace Operations'** with focus on **'Dynamics of Composition of Troops and Diversity on UN Peace Operations'**. On conclusion of each webinar, all talks are compiled and published as a Monograph to share the rich experiences of speakers with larger audience for cross fertilisation of ideas. I am happy to inform you that Monograph on **'UN Peace Operations: Hostage taking of UN Peacekeepers'** has just been published.

I express my deep gratitude to Maj Gen (Dr) AK Bardalai, Dr Chiara Ruffa, Col (Dr) KK Sharma and Col K Kekre for accepting USI's request to share their rich experience and deep insight on **'Dynamics of Composition of Troops and Diversity on UN Peace Operations'**. We are also fortunate to have a galaxy of UN professionals and practitioners participating in the event today. My special thanks to Ms Pernilla Rydén, Director of Challenges Forum, to accept our invitation to deliver Keynote Address today.

Amb Vijay Thakur Singh, DG, ICWA, is a carrier diplomat with multilateral experience during her service with Ministry of External Affairs, Government of India and who retired in Sept 2020 as Secretary (East), Ministry of External Affairs. She will make the opening remarks today.

Challenges faced in regional conflicts around the world during the 1990s called for intensified efforts to analyse and reflect on the international community's role in this new context. In this environment, Challenges Forum was launched in 1996 with the USI being a founder member. Today Challenges Forum is a global partnership of 24 countries and about 50 peace operations organisations. The Challenges Forum is a strategic and dynamic platform for constructive dialogue; and to bridge the divide between policy and operational levels; and to create shared understandings among UN and regional organisations, Member States, Troop and Police Contributing Countries; and Host Countries.

Ms Pernilla Rydén, Director, Challenges Forum International Secretariat, is a well-known UN professional with more than 20 years of experience in different international settings. She has a number of publications and reports to her credit. We are indeed fortunate to have Ms Pernilla Rydén with us today, and she will deliver Keynote Address.

Our moderator for the event today is Maj Gen (Dr) AK Bardalai who is a Distinguished Fellow at the USI and an Indian Army veteran. He has drawn rich UN experience from his earlier assignments as a UN Military Observer in Angola, a Research Fellow (UN Peacekeeping) with the

USI and as Deputy Head of the Mission and Deputy Force Commander in UNIFIL (Lebanon). He has also authored a book 'UN Peacekeeping - Changing Security Scenario: Its Implications for UN Peacekeeping'. General was awarded doctorate recently, by Tilburg University (Netherland), for his thesis on UN Peace Operations.

Opening Remarks

Amb Vijay Thakur Singh

The Indian Council of World Affairs (ICWA), India's oldest foreign policy think tank and United Services Institute of India (USI), India's oldest think tank on military affairs, have collaborated to organise a series of webinars on peacekeeping. Two webinars have already been held on the themes 'Principles of UN Peacekeeping and Mandate' and 'Hostage-taking of UN Peacekeepers'. It is my pleasure to speak at the third webinar in this series which is on 'Effectiveness of UN Peace Operations: Dynamics of Composition of Troops and Diversity on UN Peace Operations'.

Peacekeeping is a critical instrument of the UN in maintaining international peace and security. Countries contribute their troops for peacekeeping operations voluntarily. India is one of the oldest contributors to peacekeeping operations and has contributed more than 250,000 troops in 49 missions over the years, cumulatively the largest from any country. It is, thus, a vast repository of best practices. It continues to provide eminent Force Commanders for UN peacekeeping missions and has consistently been amongst the top five troop contributors of reliable and trained peacekeepers for UN peace operations since 1998. Recently, in March this year, in solidarity with UN peacekeeping, India provided 200,000 Covid 19 vaccines for UN peacekeeping personnel worldwide.

It is a reflection of India's commitment to UN peacekeeping that one of the three core issues identified during its Presidency of the UNSC in August this year was PKO. The High-Level Open-Debate on Peacekeeping at the Security Council, on August 18, on the theme of 'Protecting the Protectors: Technology and Peacekeeping', the focus was on the use of modern technological tools to enhance the safety and security of peacekeepers and to aid peacekeeping missions to implement their mandates effectively. UNSC adopted a Presidential Statement on 'Technology and Peacekeeping', the first such UN Security Council document on this topic, as also a Resolution on 'Accountability of Crimes against UN Peacekeepers'.

At the High-Level Open Debate, India's EAM announced the roll-out of the UNITE Aware Platform across select peacekeeping missions in collaboration with UN. This is a situational awareness software programme based on the expectation that an entire peace-keeping operation can be visualised, coordinated and monitored on a real-time basis. An MoU between India and the UN was also signed on training and capacity building of peacekeepers in the realm of technology.

Today, peacekeeping operations are called upon to not only maintain peace and security but also to facilitate the political processes, protect civilians, disarm combatants, support elections, protect and promote human rights, and restore the rule of law – in other words, they perform a multi-dimensional role. However, the core values of UN (UNITE Aware Platform is a technology platform for peacekeeping, https://pminewyork.gov.in/IndiaatUNSC?id=NDMyNQ) peacekeeping endure. These are - the principles of consent of the parties, impartiality, and non-use of force except in self-defence and in defence of the mandate; and these principles have guided many transitions that peacekeeping has witnessed from truce-supervision missions of yesteryears to multi-dimensional mandates of today. The UN has, over a period of time, understood the changing nature of emerging security challenges, yet there is a constant need to work towards pragmatic approaches to ensure UN peacekeeping operations continue to be effective and addresses 21th Century challenges.

The fundamental strength for the effectiveness of peace operations is the presence of well-trained and well-equipped peacekeepers, but that does not by itself lead to effective peace operations unless the peacekeepers find acceptance in the host country. Peacekeepers' acceptance by the host nation is crucial; and dependent on the host nation's perceptions of the peacekeeping contingents, which vary from contingent to contingent, its socio-cultural background, and the operational ethos of the peacekeepers.

Today's webinar will deliberate upon the impact of the composition and diversity of peace-keepers drawn from different TCCs, their varying socio-cultural characteristics, and operational behaviour patterns, on the effectiveness of UN peacekeeping operations. The importance of this factor is generally known to the practitioners but not discussed much in the academic field. Such discussions can contribute to an enhanced understanding of the issues involved on the part of researchers and enable a major TCC like India to make intellectual contributions to strengthening the effectiveness of UN peace operations.

Keynote Address

Effectiveness of UN Peace Operations – Is Diversity the Way Forward?

Ms Pernilla Ryden

Background

A lot has happened since the UN Security Council authorised the first peacekeeping mission, United Nations Truce Supervision Organisation (UNTSO), in May 1948. This peace operation consisted of a limited number of military observers who were sent to monitor a Ceasefire between Israel and its Middle East neighbours.

Until today, over one million women and men have served under the UN flag in more than 70 different peace operations. Since the end of the so called Cold War, UN peacekeeping missions have become larger, more robust, and increasingly complex. The Blue Helmets have also become more diverse, both in terms of numbers of peacekeepers and countries contributing. Today, 121 countries are contributing uniformed personnel to the 12 ongoing UN peacekeeping missions. For example, MINUSMA in Mali and UNMISS in South Sudan have peacekeepers from more than 40 different countries.

The dilemmas and challenges of UN peacekeeping in the 21st Century are much larger than before. The mandates of peace operations have further transformed from having a focus on monitoring peace agreements into a more active implementation and enforcement of peace agreements following conflicts, including civil wars. Today, peacekeepers are also increasingly being deployed where there might be: no peace to keep; a plethora of irregular armed groups, or terrorist threats – with a mandate to protect civilians.

Diversity Enhances Effectiveness

Both, research and practice shows that diversity among the Blue Helmets generally has a positive influence on the effectiveness of peacekeeping. Examples from several current UN missions suggest that cultural proximity, religious connection, and language skills are important to create a connection with the local population in the contexts where the contingents are serving[1].

Just to take one example, when a Qatari contingent joined the area under French operational control in Lebanon, under UNIFIL-flag, the civilian-military coordination in this theatre was enhanced. This was deemed to be due to the knowledge of Arabic and the Muslim identity. This shows that a cultural, language, or social connection could be assisting in enhancing communication and, slowly but surely, making progress in terms of local conflict resolution.

However, these positive results will have to be weighed against possible negative side effects such as misunderstandings between different contingents based on differences in social and cultural backgrounds; operational ethos, and variations in national military doctrines. It is important to remember that when the Blue Helmets deploy in peacekeeping missions, they carry their formations and

---

1   In 2020, the Challenges Forum hosted a webinar together with Dr. Chiara Ruffa and other scholars, on the topic of *"How diversity could affect the effectiveness of peace operations"*.

culture heritage with them. By nature, military contingents have a history and are based on the needs of their particular nation, with their own specific organisation and system within their military.

Both academic discourse and international policy show, however, that diversity among the UN troops, as well as within the mission leaderships, in most cases, increases peace operations' effectiveness. Hence, we could conclude that the output and success of a UN mission increases by enhancing diversity.

Way Forward

Reflecting on this, research shows that the diversity should be managed to minimise instances of coordination challenges and misunderstandings. Therefore, structured work is required both at the UN HQ's and mission level.

Given the above, having dynamic and ambitious peacekeepers, engaged and aware of the positive effects of diversity within UN operations, would be crucial to improve mission effectiveness in the future.

In this regard, peacekeepers might require *a more multilateral mindset* that might, to some extent, differ from the theater where soldiers and command normally operates. Creating policy and makeing more joint efforts to transform respective national military contingent should therefore be considered a priority. This could be achieved by more targeted training and exercise on the UN missions' realities on the ground. UN HQ has to ensure that the specific characteristics of troops are in line with the requirements of each peace operation.

Fast moving developments, and the use of *new technology,* make it even more important to ensure that national troops get properly trained before they are deployed into the mission area. In general, peacekeepers need to become more adaptable in order to work effectively and successfully with a diverse set of troops in the theatre of operations.

Lessons could be learnt from previous experiences, where one additional example could be taken from UNMIL in Liberia where Irish troops worked under Sweden's command. In any case, while this model might not suite all TCCs and not all environments, it is concluded that enhanced within-mission learning opportunities are likely to lead to additional positive results and, subsequently, enhance the peacekeepers performances.

In regard to streamlining efforts, ***more could also be done at UN headquarters'*** level. Relevant departments such as the Force Generation Cell or the Light Coordination Mechanism together with the Triangular Partnership (TPP) could, for example, establish a 'Task Force on Diversity' to explore common drivers and effectiveness in peacekeeping.

It is believed that different peace operations' composition of troops might be a core factor for the successfulness of the mandate implementation. Based on research, a greater output could be achieved if there are large efforts to match certain TCCs with certain mission based on skills, proximity, and geographical areas.

Another area to explore further is how ***greater diversity within Mission Leadership*** teams might lead to more legitimacy of the peace operation, both externally and internally. However, this said, geographic and other diversity might also bring potential challenges to the decision-making process within the peace operation. Hence, how to enhance cohesion within and among the Mission Leadership needs to be explored further by UN, together with partners. HQ and missions might also need to work further on developing additional capacity building for Mission Leadership.

Finally, the possibility to further explore possibilities for ***different TCCs to train together***, and in some cases, co-deploy within a specific mission theatre could be explored further for those countries who wish to do so.

The International Forum for the Challenges of Peace Operations (also called the Challenges Forum) is a global partnership covering members from 24 countries across the globe. One of the strategic objectives for the Challenges Forum is to contribute to effective implementation of development and reform of UN peace operations. One of the main tools for doing so, is to engage and discuss with partners and stakeholders, to generate new and innovative ideas. www.challengesforum.org

Dynamics of the Composition of Troops and Diversity and Military Culture - Views of an Academician

Dr Chiara Ruffa

Introduction[2]

The nature and composition of UN peacekeeping has changed dramatically over the past 20 years. In our book, Composing Peace (co-authored with Bove and Ruggeri), we identify at least three broader trends on which I would like to provide further detail. These trends are really helpful when we think about the connections between diversity and peacekeeping effectiveness (Bove, Ruffa, and Ruggeri 2020). Over the past 20 to 30 years, we see three main changes - the first one that you can see here in the graph (Fig. 1) is, there has been this very dramatic increase in the number of peacekeeping troops deployed. As you can see in this graph, uniformed UN peacekeeping personnel increased quite a lot both in terms of the number of peacekeepers deployed as you can see from the line. There has also been an increase in the number of countries supplying peacekeepers as you can see in the bin. To illustrate, the UN went from 11,000 peacekeepers deployed globally in 1989 to a little above 90,000 as of August 2018, and peaked in 2015 with a little over 10,0000 peacekeepers.

In terms of countries providing peacekeepers, we went from 46 in 1990 to 124 in August 2018.

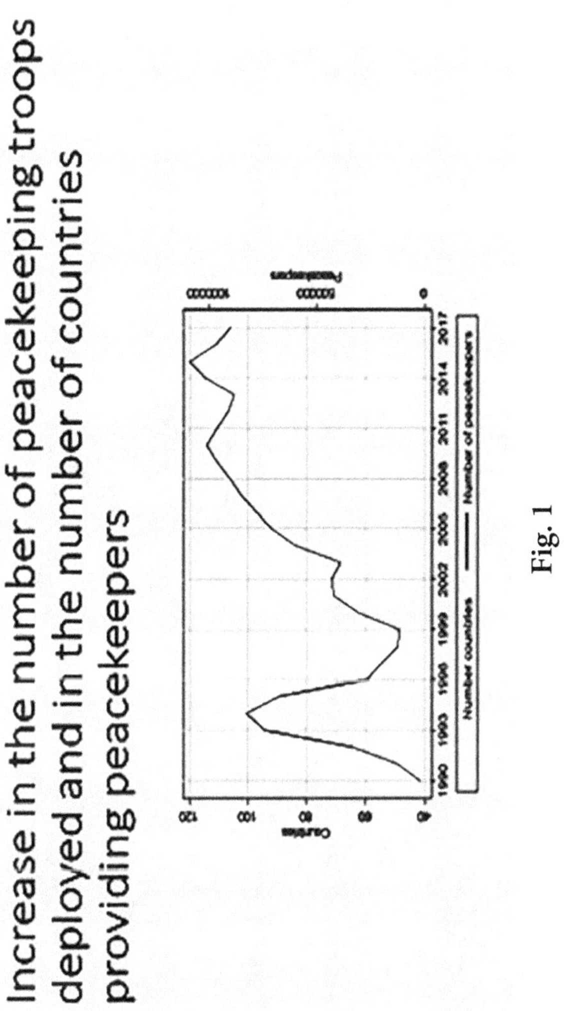

Fig. 1

The second big transformation which is important for my talk today has to do with the fact that not only we have seen a dramatic increase in the average numbers of TCCs permission but also their composition.

Different composition of countries providing peacekeepers

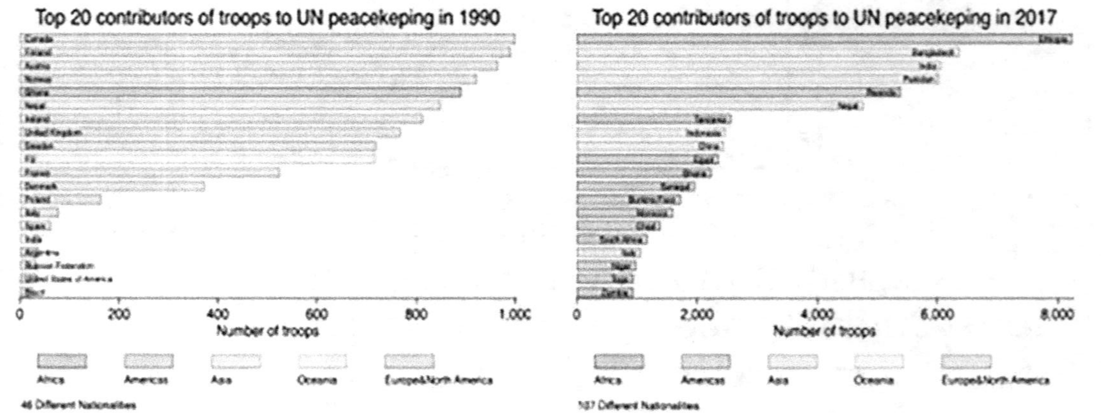

If you compare these two graphs, it is apparent that something happened between the one on the left-hand side of the slide and the one on the right-hand side. On the left-hand side we have the top troop contributors in 1990 with as you can see Canada, Finland and Austria is top three; while on the right-hand side we have the top two contributors in 2017 with Ethiopia, Bangladesh, India and Pakistan as top contributors. India continues to be one of the top contributors. Bangladesh, India and Pakistan continue to rank very high in the number of top contributing countries. This also applies to other kinds of contribution where not only the number of troops at the tactical/operational level but also when it comes to Force Commanders. We went from 157 commanders from 50 nations and we now have 97 Special Representative of the Secretary-General (SRSGs) from 50 nations, both numbers are huge increase from numbers that we have from just 20 to 30 years ago.

Another fact that I would like to mention is what the transformations in UN peacekeeping have to do with an increase in the average number of TCCs. To explain, the average number of countries in a UN African peacekeeping mission in the mid-90s were 8 TCCs. But by mid-2000, there are 21 TCCs. Just to illustrate this further, there are 56 TCCs in the UN mission in Somalia. Therefore, the missions have not only grown in size but also the number of TCCs.

Diversity and its Impact on Effectiveness of UN Peace Operations

This dramatic rise in the number of peacekeepers and the TCCs have made peace operations more diverse. In the past 30 years, UN peacekeeping missions have changed dramatically and have become much more diverse, which leads us to ask does the diversity of mission composition matters for peacekeeping effectiveness? Besides, what do we understand by the diversity of mission composition in a peace operation? Here, the focus is not on either gender or police diversity, but really about the diversity of the Blue Helmets and how does it impact the effectiveness when looked from at different dimensions. Essentially, there are four dimensions of diversity that I want to talk about:

1. Field diversity.

   (a) The diversity among the Blue Helmets deployed.

   (b) Where do the Blue Helmets come from? Does the mission consist of soldiers from two countries or a multitude?

2. Top leadership diversity.

   (a) That is the diversity between the positions of Force Commander (FC) and the Special Representative of the Secretary General (SRSG).

   (b) Is the FC Swedish and the SRSG Indian?

3. Vertical leadership distance.

   (a) That is the diversity between FC and the peacekeepers.

   (b) Does the FC lead Blue Helmets of her/his nationality or Blue Helmets from culturally, economically, or linguistically distant countries?

4. Horizontal distance.

   (a) That is the diversity between Blue Helmets and the local population

   (b) Do the peacekeepers and the local population speak the same language? Are they culturally similar?

To illustrate further, for instance, when the FC is Swedish and the SRSG is Indian or perhaps the other way around, what is the subsequent effect on peacekeeping effectiveness?

The *second* dimension of diversity we look at is about the diversity between the FC and the peacekeepers. For instance, what does it mean for an Indian FC to have a wealth of different countries to command and conversely, what does it mean for an Indian FC to have a peacekeeping force that is mainly composed of Indian peacekeepers?

Field diversity, which is the first dimension, was studied with a very in-depth exploration of three different cases. First, we looked into UNIFIL II (Lebanon) and thereafter followed by MINUSMA (Mali) and MINUSCA (Central African Republic). These are three very different kinds of peacekeeping missions that allow us to see the kind of diversity and what kind of effects does diversity have on peacekeeping missions? We found that high levels of field diversity trigger processes whereby complementarity of skills are valued and help at creating trust and willingness. It also helps to signal the UN commitment to help solve the conflict thereby it seems to also have a deterrent effect. This is very new and very important because the presence of a diverse set of Blue Helmets seems to have a distinct signalling effect which is much more than muscular deterrence and about the mere presence of peacekeeping troops. At the same time, qualitative evidence suggests that high levels of field diversity may trigger coordination problems and misunderstanding. But, overall field diversity is associated with higher levels of peacekeeping effectiveness.

Yet another connected issue is that different militaries have different operational styles. It is because along with diversity, comes a different operational style, and very different military cultures, which is what I focus on in my next session.

Military Cultures in Peacekeeping Missions

How these military cultures help shaping peacekeepers behave is very important, particularly when we have to think about several different TCCs deployed. So in my other research (Ruffa 2014; 2018a; 2017), I've dealt very deeply into a distinct body of material (combining hundreds of interviews with observations and focus groups) and more qualitative work. I have spent several months deployed with several different peacekeeping troops in the United Nations mission in Lebanon and also with several troops deployed in the NATO mission in Afghanistan. The NATO mission in Afghanistan was not UN peacekeeping but it was more a stabilisation operation with a counter insurgency twist.

It is quite interesting to find how each single peacekeeping troop interpret its mandate is very much a function of the pre-existing military culture. For my study, I interviewed French, Italian, Korean, and Ghanaian units in UNIFIL. In the case of French units, the core characteristic of the French military culture is assertiveness, which shaped the way they interpreted the mandate. By contrast, the Italian military culture was very much based on the idea of being perceived as good humanitarian soldiers. That, it was really about a fusion between long-ingrained ideas of Italian soldiers as good people and the need to reacquire a lost legitimacy from the events that had happened during World War II. This made Italian soldiers behave in a completely different way from the French. They were keener on undertaking Civil-Military Co-operation (CIMIC) projects and less on conducting patrols. In my research, the Italian and Korean military cultures are relatively similar in the sense that UNIFIL is a peacekeeping mission but different in levels of force protection. In contrast, the French military culture is current with French soldiers' perception whereby the mission was perceived and understood to be as a peace support operation.

This kind of diversity in the military culture amongst different contingents have profoundly shaped the way Italian and French soldiers behaved. For example, French soldiers did 27 patrols a day on average while the Italians did only 15. The timing of patrols was also completely different with the French mainly patrolling at night and the Italians mainly patrolling during the day. The level of armament was also very different where the French use heavy and noisy tanks while the Italians only use light Armor vehicles. So in terms of variations in force employment, we find a very big variation between Italian and French soldiers. But there was also a very distinctive variation between the Korean and Ghanaian soldiers and Italian and Korean soldiers. For instance, the Korean peacekeepers were very risk-averse, while the Ghanaian and the Indians were not because they had been in Lebanon for a long time during the UNIFIL 1 mission and also during the 2006 war. Both contingents had very close connections and very good sources for collecting and gathering information, in comparison to the French or the Korean peacekeepers.

Taken together, this finding is really important when we think about diversity because there are very distinct ways of going about when implementing the mandate. While the Italian soldiers prioritise interaction with the local population and aid projects, the French did more on patrolling and displayed higher force protection measures. This was in line with situational perceptions of French and Italian contingents deployed and the respective French and Italian military cultures.

Conclusion

So this leads me to just draw some conclusions. Just bringing together the diversity and its connection with peacekeeping effectiveness, and the military cultures, how can we reconcile, somehow, these two pieces of findings. On one hand, the fact that military cultures are really important and drive how the same peacekeeping mandate will be interpreted and understood; and on the other hand, once we know that and there are a lot of diverse forces deployed then what do we do with it? In other words, how can we go about affecting peacekeeping effectiveness?

Diversity in the UN peacekeeping mission composition is an asset and not necessarily a limitation. If considered as an asset, diversity signals the commitment of the UN and allows for the complementarity of skills. But the diversity should be managed because the military cultures produce outcomes that are just fundamentally different. Managing diversity means coordination between different contingents with diverse military cultures. But coordination between diverse contingents prompt misunderstanding. Even the knowledge of the impact of diversity helps to further explore the positive effects of diversity in terms of signalling the commitment of the UN and coordinating the complementarity of skills of the diverse contingents of the peacekeeping mission.

At the level of TCCs, it would help to make military organisations work in multinational contexts and better understand the positive effects of diversity and learn from each other. This can be achieved by making this subject part of the training curriculum more at the TCC level and less at the UN level. This would help to shift the mindset whereby peacekeepers see diversity as beneficial and not as controversial. The number of troops and technology do contribute towards improving military operations. For example, in MINUSMA there has been a lot of emphasis on high-tech institutions like Sources Information Fusion Unit (SIFU) and other intelligence-gathering agencies attached to the mission. But what is needed are soft skills like our ability to work with each other, and the ability to understand the needs of the population. Cultural variations are, therefore, likely to impact not only the effectiveness of mandate implementation but also the ability of different contingents to work together. Therefore, thinking creatively to combine different TCCs rather than the current trend of one-mission one-nation and one Area of Responsibility (AOR) concept might be more beneficial in terms of enhancing the overall effectiveness of UN peacekeeping.

References

Bove, Vincenzo, Chiara Ruffa, and Andrea Ruggeri. 2020. *Composing Peace. Mission Composition in UN Peacekeeping*. Oxford: Oxford University Press.

Ruffa, Chiara. 2014. 'What Peacekeepers Think and Do: An Exploratory Study of French, Ghanaian, Italian, and South Korean Armies in the United Nations Interim Force in Lebanon'. *Armed Forces & Society* 40 (2): 199–225. https://doi.org/10.1177/0095327X12468856.

———. 2017. 'Military Cultures and Force Employment in Peace Operations'. *Security Studies* 26 (3): 391–422. https://doi.org/10.1080/09636412.2017.1306393.

———. 2018a. *Military Cultures in Peace and Stability Operations*. Philadelphia, PA: University of Pennsylvania Press.

———. 2018b. 'Making Efforts to Improve UN Peacekeeping'. *Political Violence at a Glance* (blog). 25 July 2018. http://politicalviolenceataglance.org/2018/07/25/making-efforts-to-improve-un-peacekeeping/.

UN. 2015. 'Report of the High-Level Independent Panel on Peace Operations on Uniting Our Strengths for Peace: Politics, Partnership and People'. A/70/95–S/2015/446. New York, United States: United Nations General Assembly and Security Council.

Dynamics of Composition of Troops and Diversity - Views of a Practitioner

Colonel (Dr) KK Sharma (Retd)

Introduction

UN Peace Operations (UNPOs) have always been assessed with mixed outcomes for the past 75 years. There are operations in Palestine (UNTSO), India-Pakistan (UNMOGIP), and Cyprus (UNFICYP) lingering on endlessly as a constant reminder of unfinished agendas, even when some of the parties may not be accepting their mediations. There are many like Bosnia-Herzegovina (UNPROFOR) and Rwanda (UNAMIR) during the 1990s or in Syria, Yemen, Ukraine, and Afghanistan today, considered messy and chaotic where the older models of peacebuilding did not work. The question being asked by many scholars and diplomats is, has the time come for the UN to look at other alternatives to build peace[3]? "The factors allowing for effective peacekeeping are no more", Dunne[4] says in a write up in Nation World News, "You don't have the same factions that allow the easy creation of a ceasefire. You get into other kinds of conflicts".

The effectiveness of UNPOs was demonstrated in many missions like those in Namibia, Mozambique, Cambodia, Lebanon, and Angola. But then the major players of the UN

---

3   Nation World, July 25, 2021; https://nationworldnews.com/is-un-peacekeeping-losing-its-appeal/

4   Ibid.

Security Council and Western nations played their parts more actively than they are willing to do today.

Developing vs Developed World and UNPOs

As of 31 May 2021, Bangladesh, India, and Nepal are among the three top contributors to UN peacekeeping missions across the world. Add Ethiopia, Rwanda, Pakistan, Egypt, Ghana, and Indonesia and you have nearly 39000 (**50%**) of the uniformed peacekeeping personnel currently on the field. The general view in the available literature is that the UN peacekeeping burden falls on the troops from relatively poor, populous countries - mostly from Africa and South Asia. Western nations by comparison contribute a mere 4600 (5%).

Reasons for the Reluctance. There are many instances where the developed and many neighbouring countries had abandoned humanity from its man-made apocalypse. Cambodia and Rwanda genocides with million of deaths or starving Yemen and devastated Somalia and Syria are some of the examples. Some of the causes of this apathy as well as reluctance to contribute with the boots on the ground for UNPOs are attributed by many authors to:

➢ The theory of money from the developed world versus the working force from the developing world.

➢ No direct financial incentive for the Western countries to deploy peacekeepers.

➢ Lack of public support and popular concerns about the loss of lives. Mature democracies do care for public opinions.

➢ No direct interest and no troops on the ground.

➢ Reluctance to put their troops under UN leadership, at times considered to be sub-par.

> ➤ Involvement in bigger operations under NATO or bilateral agreements like those in Iraq, Syria, Mali, and Afghanistan.

Now that NATO and US forces are out of Afghanistan and Iraq, the debate is whether the West will engage actively with the UN and UNPOs. The French were already battling the AQIS in the Sahel and recently the UK too has committed to the United Nations Stabilisation Mission in Mali (MINUSMA), thus there is a glimmer of hope that the West will increase its presence in UNPOs.

White Man's Burden or Legacy Issues

Another side to the story is through the lens of the oft-repeated term - 'White man's burden', coined as a call to the British public by Rudyard Kipling in the late 19th Century. This is present in all the conflicts as most post-colonial era conflicts have primarily remained ethnic conflicts. These were left behind due to the colonial policies and practices in Africa and Asia. The ethnic groups struggle for independence or to be recognised as equal to each other. Colonial powers created societies by dividing them ethnically and native politicians continue to exploit the population on the same lines.

The British did not attempt to dismantle the traditional social structures that facilitate ethnic collective action (Blanton et al., 2001). There were some notable attempts at eradication of social ills but the inter-ethnic divide was too deep-rooted and maintained. It was even encouraged to rule over the masses, giving rise to the accusation of 'divide and rule' policy. Inter-religious rivalry and ethnic divides were used as an instrument of power and governance. This haunts the social fabric even now and raises its ugly head from time to time. Most of the UNPOs are largely established in such areas and there can be an equal measure of resentment or empathy on these issues.

Multicultural Communication

UNPOs are established in difficult and complex multicultural areas. The contingents and people working in these areas need to be extra sensitive to the ethnic traditions and understand the language of the land. This has been the lesson of NATO involvement in Iraq and Afghanistan, as military leaders and soldiers were not found to be sensitive to the local customs. This results in increased resentment and the rise of a volatile situation. The importance of this was realised and the US Army came out with a revised publication[5] on Cultural and Situational Understanding in 2015.

Cultures also vary and are interpreted according to interpersonal relations, concepts of time, attitudes, tolerance and authority, values, beliefs, behaviours, and norms of people in a mission area. All societies are composed of both a dynamic social structure and a culture. A social structure refers to the relations among groups of persons within a system of groups. Social structure is persistent over time and unless understood well and respected by all, can be a constant cause of tension. UNPOs are largely in such areas and all peacekeepers need to be conscious of these cultural nuances.

Diverse Ethics and Cultures

Paul and Elder (2006) defined ethics as "a set of concepts and principles that guide us in determining what behaviour helps or harms sentient creatures"[6]. We learn morals and aspects of

---

5   US – ATP 3-24.3 (2015)

6   Paul, R., & Elder, L. (2006). The Miniature Guide to Understanding the Foundations of Ethical Reasoning. United States: Foundation for Critical Thinking Free Press. p. NP. ISBN 978-0-944583-17-3.

right or wrong from our parents, teachers, novels, films, and television. Watching them, we develop a set idea of what is right and wrong, but mainly of what is acceptable. The main difference between eastern and western ethics is the fact that "Western Ethics is about finding truth"[7], whereas Eastern Ethics are "about the protocol, and showing of respect". Truth is embedded in all cultures but may have a different interpretation. Eastern ethics relates largely to family, society, and culture.

Aristotle, Chanakya and Confucius, each constructed an ethical system based on virtue and social values. Aristotle's ultimate aim was individual happiness while Chanakya focused on social well-being and Confucius's aim was on harmony. People have made their path from the guidance they have received (Refer to Table 1). Some authors call western ideas of ethics more theoretical whereas eastern ideas as more practical.

Table 1   *Comparative Analysis of Ethics: East versus West*

		Western Ethics	**Eastern Ethics**
1	Focus	Finding Truth	Protocol and Respect
2	Basis	Rational Thought	Religious teachings
3	Emphasis	Logic, Cause and Effect.	Respect towards family
4	Roots in	Athens, Rome and JudeoChristianity	Hinduism, Buddhism, Confucianism and Taoism
5	Approach	Rational	Holistic and cultural

---

7   http://www.differencebetween.info/difference-between-western-and-eastern-ethics

		Western Ethics	**Eastern Ethics**
6	Conflict and Harmony	Good must triumph over Evil	Good and Bad. Light and Dark all exist in equilibrium
7	Locus of Ethics	Aristotle placed this locus on individuals	Family and Society
8	Luke's Person or individualism	the idea of the dignity of a person	Lukes, S. (1990). Individualism. Basil Blackwell Ltd: Oxford
		the idea is autonomy - a central value for liberalism.	must learn everything from another person of his community.
		the idea of privacy. alien for ancient Greece.	Eastern cultures usually stress group harmony.
		the idea of self-development and Abstract individual.	community values - as trust, family honour.

Source: http://www.differencebetween.info/difference-between-western-and-eastern-ethics

Cultural Conflicts

Lewis (1967), the British orientalist, was the first to claim that there was a 'clash between civilisations[8]' in a speech at Johns Hopkins University in 1957. Lewis had argued that Islam and the West had differing values which would only be resolved following a conflict. Samuel P Huntington, the

---

8   Lewis, B. (1967). The Assassins: A Radical Sect in Islam. London: Weidenfeld & Nicolson.

famed political scientist, created a cult thesis as 'The Clash of Civilisation and Remaking of World Order'.

By the time of the presidential campaign in 2016, the issue of the relationship between the US and the Muslim majority world was very much in the spotlight. During the electoral process, the Republican candidate for president, Donald Trump, stated[9] (among many other things) that '*I think Islam hates us*' (Johnson & Hauslohner, 2017).

Military Organisational Culture

For the military, organisational culture plays a very critical role as it helps the force in attaining its goals. But when the military has to deal with the non-military elements, the same cultural issues may also negatively affect their effectiveness, especially when there is a 'clash' between military and non-military cultures. For contingents moving into PKO, a greater knowledge of local cultures will always help avoid offending non-combatants and the local populace (Greene et al. 2010).

In '*Military Cultures in Peace and Stability Operations*', Ruffa (2019) had challenged the widely held assumption that military contingents work similarly. Military organisational culture will always influence the behaviour of soldiers at the tactical level and contingents on PKO will always carry their own set of ethics and values with them. These may be different from other contingents. But the ethics or values may rhyme well with the similarly disposed of a country or cultural groups.

Troops and Diversity

The German research centre 'ZIF' had studied 'Regional Diversity' in 2012, calling it the "rise of the rest" and the

---

9   https://www.washingtonpost.com/news/post-politics/wp/2017 /05/20/   i-think-islam-hates-us-a-timeline-of-trumps-comments-about- islam-and-muslims/

"decline of the West". The study predicted the failure of the existing multilateral structures to accommodate the new powers, who in turn found ways to accommodate themselves – largely through a network of regional organisations. As a consequence, the UN lost its role as the major multilateral player in the area of peace operations and the Security Council is no longer the primary legitimising body for such operations.

The regionalisation may lead to more 'regional solutions for regional problems' provided the stakeholders keep the civilian population and their welfare in mind. There is always greater compatibility in terms of culture, language, operational guidelines, and interoperability amongst the regional armed forces. SADC in Mozambique and ECOWAS in West Africa or AU in Darfur and Somalia have shown that Chapter VIII can work if planned and executed properly.

Diverse Ethnicity of Conflict Areas and TCC Composition

In the existing set up of multinational UN contingents and police forces, the UNPOs need to bring all participating countries together and executing peacekeeping operations together. Diversity in UN peacekeeping missions is there to reflect upon. As per the UN DPO web, as of 31 July 2021, 87,814 peacekeepers were deployed in 12 PKO missions from 121 countries.

The ethnic composition of conflict areas and TCC composition give an interesting peep into the diversity. There is a scope to understand the ethnic fit for successful conflict resolution and UNPO composition. The top five countries and their compositions are given in Table 2.

Table 2   *Diversity in the Conflict Areas and TCCs*

#	PK Mission	Country Ethnicity	Troops Deployed	TCC Ethnicity
1	South Sudan	Traditionalist or **Christians, 18% Muslims**	*19,233 - Rwanda, India, Ethiopia, Nepal, China, Mongolia, Ghana,*	*BD, Pak* 50% Muslim troops
2	Central African Republic	**Christianity 90%, 10% Islam**	*18,343 from 10 countries,*	***6 from muslim countries***
3	Congo	**Christainity 70%, Muslim 10%**	*17,572, mix*	
4	Mali	Mande & Fula majority - Moor & Arabs; **90% Islamic faith** - Sunni	*15,134, from 10 countires,*	***50% muslim troops***
5	Lebanon	**Islam, Christianity & Judaism**	*10,561– **Indonesia,** Ghana, Nepal, India, **Malaysia,** Spain, Italy, France, China*	30% Muslim troops

Source: https://peacekeeping.un.org/sites/default/files/peacekeeping_factsheet_may_2021_english.pdf

Effect of Composition of Troops and Diversity

The study, 'Composing Peace: Mission Composition in UN Peacekeeping' has been based on four dimensions - field diversity, or the contingents diversity; top leadership diversity (FC & SRSG), vertical leadership distance, which is the diversity between Force Commander and the peacekeepers. And, the fourth dimension is the distance between Blue Helmets and the local population: a horizontal distance. Do the peacekeepers and the local population speak the same language? Are they culturally similar?

> **Diversity of Blue Helmets.** The higher the internal diversity of UN peacekeepers, the fewer civilian casualties within a conflict.

> **Leadership Diversity (SRSG and FC).** Can help mitigate civilian victimisation and battle-deaths and can be beneficial for mission effectiveness.

> **Vertical Distance.** The diversity between Force Commander and troops can have both positive and negative impact on an operation's effectiveness. Protecting civilians from victimisation rather than resolving the fighting between belligerents.

Indian Experiences of Troops Diversity

India's contributions to the effectiveness of its role in the UNPOs have been widely reported and noted for its professionalism, integrity, adhering to basic ethics, and moral values. More than 200,000 Indian troops have served in 49 out of the total 71 UNPOs mandated by the UN so far. The diversity concept can be applied in intercultural communication across these missions. Asians are widely described as embracing an "inductive speech pattern" in which a primary point is approached indirectly, but Western societies are said to use "deductive speech" in which speakers immediately establish their point (Winnie, 2003). In specific, some of India's experiences which relate to the impact of diversity and empathetic affinity to the mission populations are as follows:

> **Field Diversity and Effects.** Indian contingents' experiences have been highly positive while working with the other armies. The use of interpreters has helped in bridging the language barriers. The troops relate more closely to the developing world contingents than the advanced economies due to a perception bias. Troops have a binding reverence to places of worship and this is an important aspect of winning hearts and minds (WHAM) in these areas.

> **Leadership diversity** experience has not been very favourable at places. By and large, the FCs have maintained cordial relations with the SRSG and DPKO staff, but the difference in working styles can bring in disharmony. Examples of Sierra Leone, UNPROFOR, and ONUC can be cited to show the divergence.

> **The diversity between Force Commander and troops** has been both positive and negative on an operation's effectiveness. The need of working around the TCC governments and preventing their interference will continue to be a major challenge. Troops from the same country as FC will always be advantageous for better operational capabilities and quick response.

> Peacekeepers with **closer ethnicity to** the local population perform better due to the similarities in language and faith. Troops from locations away from the conflict areas will find the situation overwhelming and thus unable to stop the violence.

Indian Experiences in Indian Ways[10]

The effectiveness of UNPOs is dependent on multiple variables, many of these are mediating and intangibles to quantify. These will include diversity and the ability to have empathy, cultural tolerance, and alignment of basic ethics as an important part. Peacekeepers are drawn from different military doctrines, cultural and societal backgrounds. Indian contingents have always been successful in diffusing volatile situations due to their ability to go beyond the call of duty, secular credentials, and better understanding of other cultures. In 1953, after the Korean armistice agreement on the 38th Parallel, a Neutral Nations Repatriation Commission was established by the UN under the chairmanship of Lt Gen KS Thimmaya. India provided a custodian force under Maj Gen SPP Thorat, who had to keep the prisoners under closely guarded compounds. These prisoners (PoW) were then interviewed by a composite team to ascertain their willingness for repatriation to host or home country. On 24 Sep 1954, a Chinese sergeant wanted to be repatriated but others were agitated. During the ensuing dialogues, Maj Grewal, the interpreter was detained by over 200 PoW. General Thorat with 8 to 10 troops and two other officers entered the compound in a dangerous situation and attempted to calm the PoW. The CFI Commander engaged himself in conversation with one of the prisoners who spoke some English. After some time, he took out his cigarette case and asked that prisoner, *"What sort of Chinese are you? I and my men have been your guests for almost an hour but you have not seen it fit to offer a cup of tea or even a cigarette. Where is your traditional hospitality and where are your good manners for which your race is renowned"*? This broke the tension and amazed the prisoners, who immediately brought water and tea for the Indian troops and officers.

---

10   USI of India (2007). For the Honours of India.

66 (I) Brigade Group trained extensively for the mission. Somali language training was given to selected persons who worked as a bridge with the locals. The contingents adopted balanced security and humanitarian approach in their areas of responsibility. Contingents in interior areas involved village elders and clan leaders in deciding the aid and construction activities. They looked after orphanages, the veterinary unit treated animals, provided medical assistance, dug wells, and generally assisted in national infrastructure building.

Civic activities for the local population by our contingents in Lebanon, Kivu area of Congo, South Sudan, and Eritrea have been the hallmarks of the Indian approach to peace operations. The civilian population remains the centre of gravity for any operation and all-out efforts are made to work for their protection, ease of living, and creating a sense of assurance from the UN side. The best security in these far-flung areas is provided by the trust of civilians in the peacekeepers. This has been the motto and being able to empathise with the sufferings of these conflict-ridden people has helped the Indian contingents to stay the course.

Conclusion

UNPO's effectiveness is a function of clarity of UN mission mandate, appropriate force composition, maintenance of the consent by hostile parties, resoluteness of UN operational leadership, and keeping the civilian population at the centre of all activities. Indian contingents on UNPO duties will have different military doctrine, cultural and societal backgrounds, operational ethos, and outlook towards mandate implementation when compared to the other contingents in the field. But it always adheres to the Force HQ directions in letter and spirit. Keeping the civilian population at the centre of its activities, striking a balance between humanitarian and security operations have proved a successful mantra for the success of Indian peacekeepers. Well trained peacekeepers, their attitude towards the local population, and resolve to disrupt spoilers will always provide the recipe for a highly effective UNPO.

Dynamics of Cultural, Social and Military Ethos – Perspective of an Indian Contingent Commander

Colonel K Kekre

Introduction

I served in MONUSCO from 2012 to 2014 as a Logistics Staff Officer and then again as Contingent Commander from 2015 to 2016. The deployment was in the middle of the M - 23 crisis.[11] This movement was started by a rebel faction of the National Army, which led to large scale operations and major upheaval in the UN structure deployed in the mission. The mission was high octane, high visibility and had been ongoing since the year 2000 under the UN Security Council Resolution 1258 as a Chapter 7 mission.[12] The region bears the baggage of the Rwandan Genocide of 1994, where more than

---

11 The March 23 Movement (French: *Mouvement du 23 mars*), often abbreviated as M23 and also known as the Congolese Revolutionary Army (*Armée révolutionnaire du Congo*),[7] was a rebel military group based in eastern areas of the Democratic Republic of the Congo (DRC), mainly operating in North Kivu province. The 2012 M23 rebellion against the DRC government led to displacement of large numbers of people. Courtesy https://en.wikipedia.org/wiki/March_23_Movement

12 United Nations Charter, Chapter VII: Action with Respect to Threats to the Peace, Breaches of the Peace, and Acts of Aggression. Courtesy https://www.un.org

8,00,000 people were slaughtered in the Hutu – Tutsi clashes that ensued after the assassination of the Rwandan president in a plane crash. In a complex mission like MONUSCO where more than 51 countries have contributed troops, military or police, culture and values are bound to be varied and diverse. Does this diversity impinge on the efficiency of the mission mandate? Does differing military ethos pose challenges for soldiers in effective peacekeeping? If so, are there any means to bridge these differences? These are the questions that have been lingering in the minds of operational commanders and decision-makers in the UN hierarchy for long.

Culture, societal norms and ethos are the drivers of any and every society or civilisation. When this is viewed in the context of militaries, the influence is even more profound. Patriotism, discipline, procedures and drills are so interwoven in the fibre of military men that they would probably not even realise that what they are doing as muscle memory is an outcome of thousands of years of cultural baggage, social practices, traditions, and ethos which have manifested in attitudes, aspirations, and habit.

The Multinational Conundrum

In the operational canvas of MONUSCO, apart from the Indian Brigade, there was a Pakistani Brigade in the South and a Bangladeshi Brigade in the North. We had the Uruguayans, Guatemalans, Egyptians, Ukrainians, Chinese, and the newly formed Force Intervention Brigade which was composed of three African partners; Malawi, Tanzania, and South Africa. This was an extremely complex mission with multiple armed groups, a fully armed breakaway faction of the Congolese regular army, and a multi-national mission with immense diversity. If I had to identify a pattern; one could distinctly segregate them into five categories – the Latin Americans, Asians, Africans, Middle East, and

Europeans. Over some time, it was evident that the behaviour and actions of peacekeepers of all countries are governed by culture, religion, trainings, military ethos, and, last but not the least, the national agenda. The fulcrum or centre of gravity of any peacekeeping mission, however, is the local population of the host country. This is the cornerstone for the success of any military operation. Our own operational experiences back in India are replete with examples of how taking the population along has yielded disproportionate results, and also vice versa.

Let's take the example of prayers on all Tuesdays. Colloquially, the fixture has come about to be known as 'the Religious Parade', where personnel of all religions get together to pray and pay their obeisance to god as per their belief. This they follow without even realising the deep-rooted background dating thousands of years. Similarly, there are numerous examples of infusion of culture and society into the military; which is a cross-section of the same society we stay in. It is safe to assume that this would be the case with other armies across the world. For a military man serving in a multinational environment abroad, the difference in culture and ethos is distinct. If not an impediment, these differing cultural norms and societal encumbrances often create dilemmas and confusion in the minds of soldiers and pose challenges for junior leaders and functional leadership.

The dynamics of the interplay of culture, society, and military ethos in UN missions also run deep. In the succeeding paragraphs, I shall endeavour to touch upon the conflict areas and areas of convergence that military personnel encounter when deployed overseas for UN peacekeeping missions. With short tenures of six months to one year, it is difficult to assume that we can find foolproof remedial measures to overcome these challenges. However, education and mature leadership can certainly ameliorate these challenges faced in operations.

Military Manifestation of Culture

Use of Minimum Force. The primary mandate of peacekeepers in MONUSCO is to support the National Army, protect civilians, prevent sexual abuse and gender-based violence, and restore normalcy through public outreach and developmental projects. The Force Intervention Brigade is mandated to use force against armed groups in carrying out the assigned task. India as a military has matured over the years by its operational experiences back home, where it has to deal with a plethora of situations from external aggression, counter-insurgency to disaster relief. The experience has paid off and is reflected in our impeccable record in UN peacekeeping over the last seven decades. By our rich experience in North East India and Jammu and Kashmir, India has always adopted a mature approach to peacekeeping operations. The turbulence and hardships caused to the locals during the conduct of sub-conventional operations have always been mitigated by our principle of 'Iron Fist in Velvet Glove'. All sub-conventional operations are preceded and followed by mitigation of hardships, obtaining of no objection and no damage certificates, and all possible support is provided to the villagers at all times, especially during conduct of operations. More than adequate weightage is given to the safety of the civilian population and the prevention of collateral damage. Whenever the option exists between the use of heavy calibre weapons versus the use of minimum force, the latter is adopted. This template, when put into UN peacekeeping operations, has always yielded excellent results. The empathetic approach and taking the local population along also builds a sense of trust and security which is an encouraging trend in the achievement of the overall aim of restoration of normalcy.

People Friendly Operations. We, Indians, have compassion and empathy ingrained in our DNA. So, when it comes to men in uniform, the hard outer has a soft, thinking, and empathetic soldier within. This by no means impedes our professional acumen, courage, and spirit. Our military ethos in this regard have been formed and matured over the last 3-4 decades. Winning hearts and minds, people-friendly operations, and Operation Sadbhavna are certain examples of the thought process of the organisation, which manifests in action at the ground level. I will elaborate with an example from my tour of duty. We deployed our contingent, in the summer of 2015, in a place called Sake in Eastern Congo. The region was wary of prolonged operations and armed group clashes creating a humanitarian crisis; basically, misery and poverty were in abundance. The UN has an institutionalised system within its folds called the UN CIMIC or civil-military coordination.[13] One of the charters of this organisation is to provide support to the local populace in more ways than one. This is a long process involving forwarding a proposal, approval, allocation of funds, and finally execution of the projects in line with the overall thought process of the Mission Headquarters. In my case, by the time my last flight of inducting troops arrived, my Subedar Major, one morning, during our routine walks around the unit premises, took me on a detour. He wanted to show me some toilets he had created for girls studying in the local school. He had also sent some boys to assist in resuscitating the school playground; all this, within the resources at his disposal in the Unit. All he said was – "Sahab! the villagers around our camp are so poor and this is the least we can do. We will do more once our CIMIC project is approved and funds come". This is the datum at which we operate. One could pragmatically separate

---

13 Operational and tactical coordination between UN military and civilian partners in achievement of mission objectives. Courtesy https://www.unocha.org

emotion from the profession and follow the institutionalised process of help and rehabilitation which has been enunciated by the UN or add to the cause of stability and normalcy for the locals.

Secular Fabric of Indian Military.   Many of us have come across the Mandir, Masjid and Gurudwara (MMG) in units. Many units maintain MMG to cater to the religious beliefs of troops. Some units even have a Church for Christian troops. Troops in the Indian Army belong to all religions and secularity is ingrained in our ethos. The diversity extends to language, customs, and castes. However, the unity in diversity is a wonder for many who have seen it from the outside. This ability to absorb different cultures, languages, and religions extends during overseas deployment of the contingents. The troops adapt quickly and naturally. Respecting the religion and customs of the host country has greatly helped in establishing the needed connection with the locals; which is a prerequisite for sub-conventional operations. Our battalion would regularly attend the Sunday Mass at the local church; we would prepare some food and refreshments for the locals and make the event festive. The main religion of locals in Congo is Christianity and we would always join the villagers in their festivities on Christmas and New Year. Also, on Diwali, Dussehra, our Independence and Republic days, local village heads would always form part of the gathering. This was a force multiplier for our contingent as it manifested into the creation of a fantastic intelligence base and effective operations for the battalion. We were frequently informed by villagers of brewing tensions, location of armed groups, and civilians needing assistance. It helped us immensely in planning our operations, identifying localities for civic action and development projects, and projecting a positive image of the UN Forces. We would invariably hear good things about the contingent from the local population, village elders, and also from other contingents.

On Ground Connect. Another unique skill acquired by Indian troops is that on deployment to any new area, they would immediately meet with the village elders and Gaon Burhans as we colloquially call them.[14] This would help the troops in establishing the much-required connection and also for shaping the opinion of the local population. The company operating base would adopt the village, or group of villages, in its area of responsibility. The base commander would become a part of the village council as an advisor. He would empower the headman in carrying out his administration by assisting with JCB or a bulldozer once in a while, repairing an animal shed or a school playground. The Medical Officer also had a line of patients from local villages, some with livestock, who would approach with some ailment or injury every day. As Contingent Commander, I too attended cultural events in my area of responsibility. Back home, this is a common feature, especially in the North East. The troops would naturally blend with the culture of the place they are deployed in, with Congo being no exception.

Family Ties and Values. One day we received information from our local source that a one-armed group leader wanted to surrender to the UN Forces. The beat of operations of the leader of this armed group was in my area of responsibility; approximately 80 kilometre in the jungles and not connected by road. So the Formation Headquarters requisitioned a helicopter. I quickly activated a quick reaction team with a few selected boys, a language interpreter, and a local UN employee who had been employed for outreach and liaison. We flew from the battalion headquarters towards the jungle and could locate the place only after a couple of rounds over the thick forest. Once we landed, what I witnessed was humbling. More than five hundred locals had gathered with banners, flags, and drums. There was an electrifying

---

14 A village respected elder / headman/ in rural India generally part of the village administration / governance or in an advisory capacity.

atmosphere. They had come to express solidarity with their leader who was surrendering. He approached us with a group of ladies and children. We had come with a plan to extricate only the leader, and carried troops and loads accordingly in the helicopter. After a brief conversation of my interpreter with the leader, he informed me that the rebel leader insisted on taking his two wives and seven children along with him. We were taken slightly off-guard as we hadn't planned for it. However, with some permutation – the combination was worked out. His entire entourage was carried along after his repeated insistence. We had to leave some of our troops behind, whom we picked up in the next sortie to the village. So, here one could observe a fierce sense of belonging of the locals towards the leader as also of the leader for his kith and kin. He did not plan to abandon them in the village with his future uncertain.

The takeaway was that no matter how rustic, under-developed, and downtrodden the community was, family values and bonding was in abundance. The survival instinct had not diminished their ethos and values. We should be cognisant of this when we deal with locals. Give them their due, understand that they too have a culture and values which need to be respected. Identify the red lines which cannot be breached and respect them. Only then will we be able to effectively ensure peace and inculcate trust and faith in them. Also, it would take maybe years to establish the connection. Whereas, it will take only one incident of highhandedness, disrespect, or abuse which can undo years of good work. Apart from UN training, classes on the culture and tradition of the host country should be given due importance in the orientation training of potential peacekeepers.

Importance of a Socio-Cultural Connect. The social and cultural connection for a contingent deployed overseas is two dimensional. One with the population of the host country and another with other contingents deployed in the mission.

Despite the barrier of language and diverse culture, the only way one can connect and jointly operate with other contingents is through the common thread of military ethos, if not cultural. Professionalism in conduct, impeccable discipline, and a conscious effort to respect the feelings and deep-rooted values of the locals and other contingents is the only way forward. A commonality of military ideology and way of functioning brings a sense of familiarity and bonding between contingents of different nationalities.

Contingents deployed in the mission would often see small Congolese children join their hands and greet them with a 'Namaste'. Some, who have stayed close to the location of the Indian contingents over the years, even spoke Hindi. They would come to wish us on Holi and Diwali. Our troops invariably picked up colloquial Swahili words and would engage with them. This fusion of cultures is a pleasant and heartening phenomenon and indirectly lays the foundation for meaningful peacekeeping operations.

Conclusion

To conclude, I would like to quote Yuval Noah Harari in his book, 'Sapiens'. He says that it took millions of years for the human species to develop the cognitive domain of thought, rationality, separating right from wrong, value system, and traditions. Culture, values, and ethos are ever-evolving and we need to work within the gambit. More interaction on professional and social platforms, joint manship in planning and execution of operations, and collective tasking and responsibility will be the catalysts for enhanced cooperation and bonhomie while respecting each other's feelings and culture. Bilateral and multilateral exercises are an ideal means to know each other and optimise output. Finally, the onus remains on the good judgment of military leaders to be able to steer through this blurred domain and pave a way forward.

DEMOCRATIC REPUBLIC OF THE CONGO
MONUSCO
June 2019
CENTRAL AFRICAN REPUBLIC
SOUTH SUDAN
UGANDA
RWANDA
BURUNDI
ZAMBIA
ANGOLA
ITURI
NORD-KIVU
SUD-KIVU
Yaounde
Bangui
Brazzaville
Kinshasa
Matadi
Luanda
Lusaka
Kampala
Kigali
Bujumbura
Juba
Dungu
Gbadolite
Gemena
Lisala
Buta
Isiro
Mbandaka
Boende
Inongo
Ksangani
Bunia
Goma
Bukavu
Shabunda
Kindu
Lusambo
Kenge
Kananga
Tshikapa
Mbuji-Ma
Kabinda
Kalemie
Manono
Kamina
Kolwezi
Lubumbashi
BAS-UELE
SUD-UBANGI
NORD-UBANGI
MONGALA
EQUATEUR
TSHOPO
TSHUAPA
MAI-NDOMBE
SANKURU
KWILU
KASAI
KONGO CENTRAL
KWANGO
LOMAMI
KASAI CENTRAL
KASAI ORIENTAL
MANIEMA
TANGANYIKA
HAUT-LOMAMI
LUALABA
HAUT-KATANGA
HAUT-UELE
National capital
Provincial capital
Other populated place
International boundary
Administrative boundary
Main road
Secondary road
0 150 300 km
0 100 200 mi
The boundaries and names shown and the designations used on this map do not imply official endorsement or acceptance by the United Nations.
HQ MONUSCO
HQ UNPOL
GHANA
URUGUAY (+)
FPU EGYPT
FPU BANGLADESH
FPU SENEGAL
MOROCCO
NEPAL
MOROCCO
INDONESIA
INDONESIA
INDONESIA
Bunia
Bogoro
Komanda
Semliki Bridge
Kamango
Mayimoya
Mavivi
Beni
Beni Boikene
Butembo
Kiwanja
Kanyabayonga
Ndromo
Himbe
Sake
Monigi Camp
Goma
Kavumu
Bukavu
Walungu
Kamanyola
Sange
Uvira
Baraka
MOROCCO
BANGLADESH
S. AFRICA
HQ FIB
SF TANZANIA
FPU INDIA
URUGUAY
INDIA
BANGLADESH
INDIA
INDIA
CHINA
CHINA
NEPAL
FPU EGYPT
NEPAL
PAKISTAN
HQ Southern Sector
PAKISTAN
PAKISTAN
PAKISTAN
URUGUAY
NEPAL
PAKISTAN
PAKISTAN
Northern Sector
HQ BANGLADESH
BANGLADESH
BANGLADESH
MOROCCO (QRF)
MOROCCO
MOROCCO
NEPAL (-)
FPU INDIA
BANGLADESH
MALAWI
S. AFRICA
TANZANIA
TANZANIA
S. AFRICA
BANGLADESH
INDONESIA
TANZANIA (+)
TANZANIA (+)
BANGLADESH
HQ Central Sector
HQ Force
HQ MALAWI
INDIA
LOG URUGUAY
INDIA
S. AFRICA
S. AFRICA
UKRAINE
FPU SENEGAL
INDIA (+2)
BANGLADESH
SF GUATEMALA
MALAWI
TANZANIA
Lake Albert
Lake Edward
Lake Kivu
Lake Victoria
Lake Tanganyika
10°N
0°
10°S
20°E
30°E
0 20 40 km
0 20 40 mi

Diversity in UN Peace Operations: A Challenge to Effectiveness?

Major General (Dr) AK Bardalai (Retd)
(Moderator)

Introduction

With the increasing number of complex intra-state conflicts, the relevance of UN peace operations has come under the scanner. This is so, even though there is enough literature to prove that the UN has been effective in bringing peace and reduce the bloodshed. On its part, the UN has made a sincere effort to introduce some reforms to enhance the effectiveness of peace operations. Mandates have become stronger and peacekeepers are better trained and well equipped than earlier. Despite that, peace operations continue to come under criticism with demand to make it more effective. The question, therefore, is that is there anything else that must be considered to make these peacekeepers more effective in addition to enhancing their capability. Or is that our understanding of effectiveness itself needs more explanation?

Effectiveness

The word effectiveness can be confusing. There is no fixed definition of mission effectiveness.[15] In the context of UN

---

15   Lise Morje Howard, *Power in Peacekeeping* (New York: Cambridge University Press, 2019), 9, 100. Also see Joseph R. Matthews, "Assessing Organisational Effectiveness: The Role of Performance Measures," *The Library Quarterly* 8, no. 1 (2011): 83-110. J. Soeters,

peace operations, apart from the periodic UN Secretary-General's report to the Third Committee of the UN General Assembly and the UNSC, there are no objective criteria to measure the effectiveness of any peace operation.[16] Different organisations use different measures to assess their achievements and effectiveness. There is also confusion in differentiating between effectiveness and efficiency, and the interpretation of the relationship between effectiveness and efficiency. For instance, despite a mission comprising capable and well-equipped peacekeepers, it may still not be effective on the ground. For example, Howard observed that even though peacekeepers are not consistent in achieving their intended goals, by most assessments, peacekeeping is effective.[17] To elaborate further, a capable quick reaction force (QRF) may not be able to take control of a sensitive situation in time because of the adverse effect of the underdeveloped terrain on its mobility. On the other hand, despite a good communication network, an inefficient QRF may not be effective to control a similar situation.

Diversity and Effectiveness

The effectiveness of a UN peace operation can be judged from their achievement of set targets or goals. But, the multiple variables make it difficult to measure the effectiveness of a peace operation in achieving its goals. There are also a few scholars who consider the contribution of the peace

---

Management and Military Studies. Classical and Current Foundations (London/New York: Routledge), 2020.

16 The Social, Humanitarian and Cultural Affairs Committee of the UN General Assembly is also known as 'Third Committee'.

17 Lise Morje Howard, "Power and United Nations Peacekeeping," *Power in Peacekeeping* (New York: Cambridge University Press, 2019), 1-3.

operation to create negative peace as effective.[18] UN peace operations are like military operations. But, since the UN peacekeeping force comprises a diverse force with distinct cultural and social behaviour, its effectiveness will be difficult to be judged without assessing diverse behaviour impact on the ground.[19] Because distinct military cultures of different military units, which shape their behaviour, when employed in multinational operations, in turn, can affect the outcome of peace operations. For instance, that different levels of diversity and distances can be advantageous as well as create organisational challenges and coordination problems to and for peace operations.

Participation in peace operations is by choice. Hence, the composition of the mission will vary from one mission to another with different diverse effects depending on the troops that participate. Once equipped with the knowledge of how social behaviours of peacekeepers can affect the performance of peace operations, it is important to learn how to use this information by the practitioners as well as the local populace where lies the centre of gravity of a successful peace operation. The practitioners should know how their behaviour is perceived by the recipient and, accordingly, sensitise the host nation that the unique behaviour of peacekeepers is based

---

18   Vincenzo Bove, Chiara Ruffa and Andrea Ruggeri, *Composing Peace: Mission Composition in UN Peacekeeping* (New York: Oxford University Press, 2020), 25; Annemarie Peen Rodt, "Successful Conflict Management by Military Means," *Ethnopolitics,* 11, no. 4(2012): 376-91; Lise Morje Howard, "Peacekeeping, Peace Enforcement and UN Reform." *Georgetown Journal of International Affairs,* 16, no. 2(Summer/Fall 2015): 9, http://www.jstor.org/stable/43773690

19   Chiara Ruffa, "Force Employment, Unit Peace Operation Effectiveness, and Military Cultures," *Military Cultures in Peace and Stability Operations: Afghanistan and Lebanon* (Philadelphia: University of Pennsylvania Press, 2019), 21.

on their social culture and is not offensive. Sensitising or trying to change the minds of the local populace is difficult because this task itself can be considered intrusive. Besides, the people of the host nation are more likely to be averse to the idea of being instructed by outsiders. There was an instance in Lebanon in June 2007, when the peacekeepers who wanted to implement the mandate in all sincerity but not being able to adapt to the situation fell victim to the attack of the armed groups. It was simply because the behaviour of this contingent, from one of the western nations, was considered arrogant and offensive. The resultant death of the peacekeepers forced the contingent to mend their ways and was probably not as effective as earlier fearing retaliation from the rogue elements. It is not about only adapting to the ground and making peace operations more effective. Rather than looking at the challenges related to diversity, it should be seen in the context of other closely related variables that similarly contribute to making peace operations effective. Two such factors are strategic communications and mission leadership.

Strategic Communications

Much as one would like to expect the peacekeepers to condition their social behaviour, the short stay in the field is a limiting factor. This often results in negatively shaping the perception of the host, further increases the social distance, and armed groups trying to malign the peacekeepers with a disinformation campaign. Even the High-Level Independent Panel on Peace Operations (HIPPO) noted that, "UN Peace Operations often struggle to communicate their messages to the local population and broader global community".[20] To counter this, the UN uses strategic communications to

---

20 UN General Assembly Security Council, *High Level Independent Panel Report*, A/70/95–S/2015/446 (June 17, 2015).

reach out to diverse stakeholders to build trust and to deter potential spoilers. It essentially means, "The purposeful use of communications by an organisation to fulfil its mission".[21] Given the importance of strategic communication, in the UN there is a shift from public information to strategic communication. In the 2000s, Strategic Communication Division was created and in 2020, a global communication strategy was created. Now, the Department of Public Information (DPI) has been renamed as Department of Global Communications. Such a strategy, however, is not without drawbacks. There is always a gap between UN rhetoric and action. More often, the communicators are unable to communicate what they should and what they want to communicate. Besides, there are several external and internal challenges to why strategic communication may not work. Currently, most of the missions try to operationalise the communication strategy. One of the internal challenges is the social behaviour of the peacekeepers. At this, let me give two examples from my experience.

One, the CIMIC teams from the developed nations are specially trained to undertake outreach activities and don't undertake operational activities. In any incident of relationship with the local population, which may take place because of the behavioural problem of the peacekeepers, it is the CIMIC team experts who reach out to the public to resolve the issue amicably. By and large, the strength of such experts is over and above the UN-authorised strength. In contrast, most of the contingents from the Global South deploy with their authorised strength and are generally

---

21 Jake Sherman and Albert Trihart, "Strategic Communications in UN Peace Operations: From and Afterthought to an Operational Necessity," *International Peace Institute*, August 19, 2021, https://www.ipinst.org/2021/08/strategic-communications-in-un-peace-operations

multitasking. In a similar incident which could be the result of a behavioural problem, the same peacekeepers who are out on operational duties reach out to the aggrieved party and resolve the issue. The aggrieved party, in turn, is happier to hear the word 'sorry' from the ones who were the cause of the problem even if it was without intent rather than 'sorry' outsourced to some experts.

Two, a small incident that took place in Lebanon sometime in 2008. It so happened that one of the senior Indian military staff from the UNIFIL HQs was travelling by road from Sector East to UNIFIL HQs. Halfway through his journey, he was overtaken by a speeding car with young Lebanese boys in it. The boys yelled at him and gestured with their hands. The gestures were neither offensive nor vulgar but were as if challenging the officer to beat them in the race. The UNIFIL officer did not react and kept driving at his speed. After a while, he came across the same Lebanese vehicle waiting for him and then overtaking him again with similar gestures. The officer could not be provoked and this game continued. After a while, the officer again came across the vehicle but this time parked on the side of the road with the engine switched off. As the officer crossed them, they waved at him with a smile and gesturing him to move ahead. The young Lebanese probably wanted to tell the UNIFIL officer that that is their land and they have the right to do what they wanted to do. And, the UNIFIL officer's not taking their challenge was considered as the foreigner accepting their rights. They were happy and waved him off. Communication is also a skill that comes only with training and experience. To the Indians, it seems to come naturally.

Leadership

Different social behaviours, as we have observed, have their strength and weaknesses. To take the best out of the peacekeepers will depend on the mission leaders' deep comprehension of the operational dynamics of the mission. UN peace operations are military operations but with the UN mandate to operate outside the contingents' home state. Defining command of military force, King mentioned that, "Command consists of three intimately connected functions: mission objective, mission management and mission motivation".[22] He further went on to state that these three elements are inseparable and the leader who can define these competently is also able to motivate his troops. Like all military operations, the peacekeeping force is led by a Force Commander (FC) who is a uniformed man. But barring two missions, the head of the mission (HoM) is a civilian UN employee who is generally the Special Representative of the Secretary-General (SRSG). These senior mission leaders don't have an enviable task primarily for two reasons. *One*, the decision-making process in the complex politico-military environment is complex and challenging. *Two*, even though the HoM draws his authority from the Secretary-General based on the UN charter, the command and control are generally not like the military command channel.

Even the FC faces similar challenges of mission management and mission motivation, primarily because of the participation in peacekeeping by choice and the general disliking in the UN towards the words *command and control*. Therefore, command and control are more of a product of coordination, cooperation, and management. In a diverse force, good comprehension of the challenges and how to get the best out of the contingents is the art of leadership. For instance, UNIFIL is one unique mission where the diversity is between the contingents from the western and non-western nations. Some of the contingents are equipped with advanced

---

22   Antony King, "Defining Command," *Command: The Twenty-First Century General* (Cambridge: Cambridge University Press, 2019), 69

weapon systems which are rare in UN peacekeeping. Useful employment of these capable peacekeepers from the west, and skilled peacekeepers from the non-western nation, depends on the prevailing circumstances as well as the ingenuity of the mission leaders. This apart, even the other leadership traits such as ability to take risks contribute towards the effectiveness of peace operations.

In the UN integrated missions, SRSG is the top political representative of the Secretary-General who is expected to play a coordinating role inside as well as outside the UN. Karlsrud noted that the mission leaders have to navigate in unchartered waters and operate between conflicting parameters of adherence to norms and principles of peacekeeping and deliver in the fields. He went on to state that, "The rules and norms of an organisation are more than bounded rationality, distinct from the environment — they shape the rationality of the organisation's actors and guide individual action".[23] When it comes to taking a crucial decision, the leader interprets the mandate according to his interpretation of the UN charter and in terms of personal gain or loss of prestige. While some leaders calculate the loss should the decision becomes counterproductive, there are examples of SRSGs who risked their political careers to save innocent lives. For instance, as mentioned earlier, in Bosnia, the leaders, despite having the resources at hand, refused to call the airstrike by NATO when the Bosnian Serbs killed thousands of unarmed civilians and took Dutch peacekeepers hostage[24]. In contrast, in Rwanda, Gen

---

23 John Karlsrud, "Special Representatives of the Secretary-General as Norm Arbitrators? Understanding Bottom-up Authority in UN Peacekeeping," *Global Governance*, no.19(2013), 525-544

24 Michael N. Barnett and Martha Finnemore, "The Politics, Power and Pathologies of International Organizations," *International Organizations*, 53, no. 4 (Autumn 1994): 725.

Dallaire, the FC and his staff risked their lives to save as many as innocent Rwanda civilians from the genocide by the Hutu in April 1994[25]. Similarly, in 2005, the UN Stabilisation Mission in Haiti (MINUSTAH) fired more than 20,000 rounds of ammunition, grenades and mortar fire and killed the gang leader Emmanuel "Dread" Wilme and many of his followers[26]. Likewise, in April 2011, in Cote d'Ivoire, when the country's internal situation was going out of hand because of violence perpetrated by Defence and Security Forces of Cote d'Ivoire (FDSCI), the UN along with French Licorne forces attacked with heavy weapons, entered the presidential palace and captured President Gbagbo[27]. Even if Rwanda was considered a failure, the FC was effective in saving hundreds of lives. Similarly, the leaders in Haiti and Cote d'Ivoire took risks to implement the mandate. Essentially, it is individual leadership characteristics that can be the turning point in the trajectory of peace operations.

Conclusion

Participation in peace operations is by choice. Since participation by troops from the developed nation is either negligible or selective, the current trend of participation from the Global South would continue making the composition of a peacekeeping mission geographically diverse. Along with geographical diversity comes cultural, traditional, religious, and linguistic diversity. This presents a challenge to effective coordination amongst the peacekeeping contingents to enhance the performance of the peacekeeping mission.

---

25 Romeo Dallaire, *Shake Hands with the Devils,* (Cambridge: Da Capo press, 2005)

26 Colum Lynch, "UN Peacekeeping More Assertive, Creating Risk for Civilians," *Washington Post,* 15 August 2005.

27 John Karlsrud, "Special Representatives of the Secretary-General as Norm Arbitrators? Understanding Bottom-up Authority in UN Peacekeeping," *Global Governance,* no.19(2013), 525-544

However, along with the challenges of diversity comes a multinational peacekeeping mission. Multilateralism and unilateralism, however, can be competitive. Even then, since peacekeeping is the collective responsibility of the member states, a multinational force, provided it is steered well and effectively coordinated, has a better chance to produce at least negative peace. At the same time, multilateralism should not be limited only to a multinational force but expanded to the multinational policy making system. Currently, this domain is controlled by a small multilateral alliance of the P 3 members of the P 5 members (the US, France and UK), which is unlikely to change anytime soon.

Closing Remarks

*Major General BK Sharma, AVSM, SM** (Retd)*

I begin with gratitude to Mrs Singh for having very patiently sat through the whole proceedings. My compliments to Major General PK Goswami, Major General AK Bardalai, and Ms Paernila Ryden, Director Challenger Forum for making the event a big success. I am grateful to Professor Ruffa, Colonel KK Sharma, and Colonel K Kekre for their insightful expositions.

Today's discussions have reinforced my observations as former UNMO with UNITED NATIONS OBSERVER GROUP IN CENTRAL AMERICA (ONUCA) - a mission in Central America, wherein, we were inter alia involved in the disarming and demobilisation of CONTRAS. Bases in Honduras were being used by the US to supply military arsenal to CONTRAS against SANDINISTAS. ONUCA comprised UN peacekeepers from about 12 countries and the mission expanded beyond Nicaragua to the remaining four countries of Central America. The mission entailed creation of a demilitarised zone in Nicaragua, demobilisation, disarming, and rehabilitation of armed guerrilla cadres. Besides the UN, the other stakeholders included a host of government agencies, the Organisation of other American States (OAS), the Church, and NGOs. This experience was unique in the sense that the lessons learnt from the ONUCA mission may be applied for a future mission in Afghanistan.

Most UN missions have peacekeepers and allied support systems drawn from diverse backgrounds. What stood out clearly from today's discussions is that diversity in UNPKO has some challenges but if managed well, it is a boon that is fundamental to the upkeep of the cosmopolitan character and culture of Blue Helmets.

We look forward to more such invigorating discussions in times to come. To this end, a collaboration between the USI, ICWA, Challenger Forum, NUPI, EPON, and other research and policy institutions will be a great step forward. USI was consulted by the High Level Independent Panel on UN Peace Operations (HIPPO) panel on the UN reforms. We have a very rich resource faculty; most of us have been in the UN mission, then other force commanders are associated with the USI in their capacity as our life members. Mrs Vijay Thakur Singh herself has been at our UN Mission in New York and presently heading the ICWA. Likewise, India's CUNPK is one of the most accomplished regional nodes for capacity building in the UNPKO. So it is high time that we put our heads together and provide a much needed global platform for the cross-fertilisation of ideas on doctrinal issues and policy review and reforms The very character and the nature of UN peacekeeping operations has undergone a dramatic change. Today, we are operating in the grey zone environment in multi-domains. There are no clear-cut friends and foes, state and non–state actors and crime cartels seamlessly intermingle. Peacekeeping operations have come to be characterised by volatility, uncertainty, complexity, and ambiguity. Technology has added a new dimension to the planning and prosecution of UNPKO. Digitisation of UNPKO is the direction to be adopted to enhance operational effectiveness.

I think peacekeeping is a very narrow concept, today you have to look at peacebuilding. In this regard, conflicts in Syria, Iraq, and Afghanistan offer good lessons. While one may de-conflict the country for some time but if peacekeeping effort is not supplemented by humanitarian assistance and peacebuilding, the conflict will reappear sooner than later, in one form or the other. The durable peace will remain elusive. UN has great scope in peacebuilding even in Afghanistan. We should look at this challenge collectively and work on making a 360-degree assessment, possible scenarios, and recommendations on constructing and implementing a mandate in Afghanistan. It is high time that we transform the UN from reactive to proactive conflict prevention and proactive management institution. It would be in the fitness of things that we conduct tabletop exercises on these topical conflict-ravaged countries. USI has a proven niche in scenario gaming that Director CUNPK and partner institutions may like to harness for future deliberations.

You will be happy to know that after each webinar, we prepare Monographs with an intent to synthesise these in the form of books to be introduced as reading material at different UN peacekeeping centres. Our collaboration can add to seminal literature on the UN issues for wider circulation and debates.

So with these words, I thank you all once again and we look forward to future exciting sessions.